What to Do When Your Prayers Seem Unanswered

Andrew Wommack

© Copyright 2023 – Andrew Wommack

Printed in the United States of America. All rights reserved. No portion of this book may be reproduced, stored in a retrieval system, or transmitted in any form or by any means—electronic, mechanical, photocopy, recording, scanning, or other—except for brief quotations in critical reviews or articles, without the prior written permission of the publisher.

Scripture quotations are from the King James Version. All emphasis within Scripture quotations is the author's own.

Published in partnership between Andrew Wommack Ministries and Harrison House Publishers.

Woodland Park, CO 80862 - Shippensburg, PA 17257

ISBN 13 TP: 978-1-5954-8572-4

For Worldwide Distribution, Printed in the USA

1 2 3 4 5 6 / 26 25 24 23

Above All Things

To anyone who knows the Lord or desires to know the Lord, communication with Him is essential. That's what prayer is. It's simply talking to the Lord. It's not a monologue but a conversation where we speak to the Lord, and He speaks back to us.

In Matthew 7:7, Jesus told us to ask (and we would receive), to seek (and we would find), to knock (and doors would open for us). He went on to say in verse 8 that everyone who asks receives, everyone who seeks finds, and everyone who knocks would have the door opened to them.

But that doesn't seem to match our experience.

I'm sure you've petitioned the Lord for something before and didn't see the manifestation of what you asked Him for. Therefore, it's obvious that He doesn't answer every prayer, isn't it?

But there is another way to view this. That's why I've titled this booklet *What to Do When Your Prayers **Seem** Unanswered*. The emphasis is on the word *seem*.

The truth is that the Lord always answers all our prayers that are based on a promise He has given us in His Word. 1 John 5:14–15 says,

And this is the confidence that we have in him, that, if we ask any thing according to his will, he heareth us: And if we know that he [hears] us, whatsoever we ask, we know that we have the petitions that we desired of him.

God's Word is His will. So, when we ask anything according to a promise in His Word, we can rest assured that He has heard us and that we have what we've asked for.

There are some qualifications on asking and receiving, such as in James 4:3, which says,

Ye ask, and receive not, because ye ask amiss, that ye may consume it *upon your lusts.*

The Lord loves us so much that He won't give us things that are bad for us.

And Mark 11:24 says,

Therefore I say unto you, What things soever ye desire, when ye pray, believe that ye receive them, *and ye shall have* them.

We have to believe that we receive what we ask for when we pray, not when we see it—and then we *shall* have it. This reveals that we have to have faith when we pray in order to receive. Jesus said in Matthew 21:21–22,

Jesus answered and said unto them, Verily I say unto you, If ye have faith, and doubt not, ye shall not only do this which is done *to the fig tree, but also if ye shall say unto this mountain, Be thou removed, and be thou cast into the sea; it shall be done. And all things, whatsoever ye shall ask in prayer, believing, ye shall receive.*

We have to ask for things that are promised in God's Word, and we have to believe we receive when we pray. But like you, I've asked for things I know were promised in God's Word and didn't see them come to pass. For instance, 3 John 1:2 says,

Beloved, I wish above all things that thou mayest prosper and be in health, even as thy soul prospereth.

You can't make it any clearer than that. It's God's will for us to prosper and be in health just as much as it's His will for us to prosper in our souls. Yet there are times I've prayed for prosperity and healing and didn't see any difference.

> It's God's will for us to prosper and be in health just as much as it's His will for us to prosper in our souls.

What's Going On?

I believe what God's Word says, but I also can't deny what I see and feel. How can these things be reconciled?

<u>There is a simple way to reconcile what God's Word says with what we see and feel. And for me, the key is found in the book of Daniel.</u>

Daniel was a powerful man of God who served the Lord while the Jews were in captivity to the Babylonians, Medes, and Persians. He had interpreted Nebuchadnezzar's dream

(Dan. 2), the handwriting on the wall (Dan. 5), and was delivered from the lion's den (Dan. 6). Daniel was no novice.

Yet, Daniel didn't get the same results every time he prayed and asked things of the Lord.

For instance, in Daniel 9, Daniel prayed and asked the Lord for understanding of Jeremiah's prophecy about the Jews' seventy years of captivity. He began his prayer in Daniel 9:4 and continued down through Daniel 9:19. It only takes about three minutes or less to read that prayer, so it was a short prayer for him to offer up. But while Daniel was still praying, the angel Gabriel appeared and told Daniel he was sent to answer Daniel's prayer and give him the understanding he was seeking. That's awesome! If the Lord interrupted all of our prayers with the answer, I'm sure we would love that.

But in Daniel 10, we see Daniel praying another prayer with totally different results. In that instance, Daniel prayed and fasted, and it took three weeks for a messenger to appear and give him his answer (Dan. 10:1–11).

This begs the question, **"Why did it take three minutes in Daniel 9 but three weeks in Daniel 10?"**

<u>That question is all wrong.</u> The Lord didn't answer one prayer in three minutes and the other prayer in three weeks. It looked that way from our human perspective, but that wasn't what happened at all. A failure to understand this lies at the heart of one of the major hindrances to receiving from the Lord.

Without instruction, we only believe what we can see or feel with our physical senses. That's the way we were all raised. We weren't taught to believe in the unseen realm; but the truth is that there's a lot going on in the spiritual realm that we can't perceive with our physical senses.

Look at Daniel 9:23. While Daniel was still praying, the angel Gabriel told him that the Lord had commanded at the beginning of his prayer to go and give Daniel the understanding he was seeking.

> *At the beginning of thy supplications the commandment came forth, and I am come to shew* thee; *for thou* art *greatly beloved: therefore understand the matter, and consider the vision.*

The truth is that it didn't take the Lord three minutes to answer Daniel's prayer in Daniel 9 and three weeks to answer his prayer in Daniel 10. The Lord answered both prayers instantly. Look at Daniel 10:12:

> *Then said he unto me, Fear not, Daniel: for from the first day that thou didst set thine heart to understand, and to chasten thyself before thy God, thy words were heard, and I am come for thy words.*

These scriptures reveal that the Lord answered both of Daniel's prayers at the beginning of his supplication, although the period of time it took for Daniel to receive the answers varied greatly.

Instant Prayer?

To understand this, we have to get rid of some of our religious thinking. Most of us have the idea that if God wills something to happen, it just happens instantly—that there is no such thing as time or distance or resistance to what God wills. But that's not what these scriptures reveal.

In Daniel 9, the Lord spoke to Gabriel at the beginning of Daniel's prayer, yet it took about three minutes for Gabriel to show up. That's not a long time, but it does show that from the time the Lord gave the command to the time Daniel received his answer involved time. It's possible that Gabriel was on the other side of the universe, and it took him three minutes to travel many light years. I don't know what the delay was, but the Lord answered Daniel at the beginning of his prayer, yet it was about three minutes before Gabriel gave Daniel his answer.

So again, the assumption that things happen instantly when the Lord gives the command isn't what these scriptures teach us. Even Jesus experienced this. Jesus healed ten lepers in Luke 17:12–19, but it didn't manifest instantly. It happened as they went to show themselves to the priest for their cleansing.

That verse I've already used in Mark 11:24 says that we have to believe we receive when we pray, and then we *shall* have it. That implies time. I don't think it has to take a long time, but it often does take some time.

That's what happened to Daniel in Daniel 10. Verse 12 says that from the first day Daniel prayed, the Lord gave the command to His messenger to give Daniel his answer. But in that instance, there was demonic opposition to the messenger of the Lord. The messenger was sent instantly, but he didn't arrive to enlighten Daniel until three weeks had gone by.

The Lord wasn't the variable in either of the answers to Daniel's prayers. He was the same (Heb. 13:8). But there was a demonic power that opposed the messenger bringing Daniel his answer. Daniel 10:13 says,

But the prince of the kingdom of Persia withstood me one and twenty days: but, lo, Michael, one of the chief princes, came to help me; and I remained there with the kings of Persia.

This "prince of the kingdom of Persia" was describing a demonic power that operated in the unseen, spiritual realm. Ephesians 6:12 says,

For we wrestle not against flesh and blood, but against principalities, against powers, against the rulers of the darkness of this world, against spiritual wickedness in high places.

Satan can hinder the manifestation of our answered prayers like he did with Daniel. If we don't understand that and continue with the false idea that once the Lord commands an answer, it just happens instantly, then our faith will falter when we don't see immediate results.

What if Daniel had given up on the twentieth day? He could have thought, *I got an answer in three minutes last time. This time it's nearly three weeks. God must not have answered my prayer.* If Daniel had done that, I believe he wouldn't have seen his answer, although God's answer was on the way.

Once again, Jesus said in Matthew 21:21 that we had to believe and doubt not. Paul also said in Galatians 6:9,

And let us not be weary in well doing: for in due season we shall reap, if we faint not.

The "if we faint not" is crucial to this promise. If Daniel had wavered in his faith, he would not have received anything of the Lord (James 1:7); but that wouldn't have been because the Lord didn't move. It would have been because Daniel gave up on his prayer.

The battle that was waging in the heavenlies would have been lost if Daniel had withdrawn his faith (Eph. 3:20; Heb. 10:23). Sadly, that's what happens to us many times. The Lord is faithful to His Word and commands the answer to our prayers, but they can be hindered and take time to manifest. The answer is on the way; but if it's hindered, we often give up and stop the manifestation.

Believing Is Seeing

The truth is, the Lord answered Daniel's second prayer exactly the same as He did the first prayer. The difference wasn't God but the devil. There was a battle going on in the spiritual realm that Daniel couldn't see. And this leads us to another false assumption most people have, which stops us from receiving. Most people believe that only what they can see, taste, hear, smell, and feel is real. If they can't perceive it with one of these five senses, then it doesn't exist. That's wrong.

There is a whole spiritual realm that exists, which we can't perceive with our limited senses. You've never seen or felt TV and radio signals, but they do exist. All you have to do to prove it is turn on a receiver. Seeing and hearing the broadcast is not when the station starts the broadcast. Those signals already exist. They are just in a realm we can't perceive with our five senses.

Look at what happened with Elisha and his servant in 2 Kings 6. Elisha was receiving revelations from the Spirit of the Lord about the king of Syria's battle plans. He shared these revelations with the king of Israel and therefore, the Syrians were always defeated.

When the king of Syria found out how the king of Israel was always able to know his strategies, he sent his armies to capture Elisha in the town of Dothan. When Elisha's servant arose early one morning, he discovered they were totally surrounded by the Syrian armies. He knew why they were there, and he said to Elisha in 2 Kings 6:15b,

Alas, my master! how shall we do?

That's the *King James Version*'s way of saying he panicked. But how did Elisha respond?

And he answered, Fear not: for they that be *with us are more than they that* be *with them.* (v. 16)

Most people would consider that a bald-faced lie. You could count the Syrians by the thousands, and there were only Elisha and his servant. That would have been a lie if the only things that are real are what you can see, taste, hear, smell, and feel. But there is a real, spiritual realm that exists beyond our senses.

Those who don't believe anything exists outside of what we can perceive with our senses are what the Bible calls "carnal." Romans 8:6–7 says,

For to be carnally minded is *death; but to be spiritually minded* is *life and peace. Because the carnal mind* is *enmity against God: for it is not subject to the law of God, neither indeed can be.*

Those who are only controlled by their senses are not dealing with all of reality. God is a Spirit (John 4:24), and to truly worship Him, we have to contact Him in spirit and in truth. Romans 8:8 goes on to say that those who are in the flesh (controlled by their senses) cannot please God. We have to walk by faith and not by sight only (2 Cor. 5:7).

So, those who confess they are healed when they still feel sick are not lying. They are just taking into account what is true in the spiritual realm. They don't deny the physical realm. They just deny that the physical is all there is. There is a born-again spirit inside of all true believers that has the resurrection power of Jesus in it. That power is voice activated (Prov. 18:21; Ps. 91:2), and as we express our faith through our words, what is true in the spiritual becomes true in the physical.

Faith is like a bridge between these two realms. You could also imagine faith to be like a pipe through which what is true in the spiritual has to flow through to get into the natural (physical). If that pipe is clogged or bridge is broken, then God's answer in the spiritual realm can't get into the physical realm.

Elisha's servant was going only by what he could see in the physical realm. In the natural, they were totally outnumbered. But in the spiritual realm, the Syrians were outnumbered.

2 Kings 6:17 says,

And Elisha prayed, and said, LORD, I pray thee, open his eyes, that he may see. …

I guarantee you Elisha wasn't praying that his servant's physical eyes would be open. That was his problem. His physical eyes were wide open, beholding the problem. He was totally dominated by what he saw with his eyes.

Elisha prayed that the Lord would allow his servant to see with his spiritual eyes, or as Paul prayed in Ephesians 1:18 with *"the eyes of your understanding…"*. We can see things with our heart that we can't see with our physical eyes. We can walk by faith and not be limited to our sight (2 Cor. 5:7).

2 Kings 6:17 goes on to say,

And the Lord opened the eyes of the young man; and he saw: and, behold, the mountain was full of horses and chariots of fire round about Elisha.

Praise the Lord! What Elisha said about there being more with them than with the Syrian army was true. It just wasn't true if all you acknowledge is the physical realm (i.e., what you can see, taste, hear, smell, and feel). But if you take all of reality into account, which includes the spiritual realm, it was absolutely true that God's angels (who were with them) far outnumbered the soldiers in the Syrian army.

Wow! It's the same with us. We may be faced with overwhelming odds in the natural realm, but in the spiritual realm, every believer has access to God's limitless power and ability. It's there, but we have to have faith to bring it into the physical realm. It isn't automatic.

> Every believer has access to God's limitless power and ability.

The angels didn't come to the mountains to surround them once Elisha's servant had his spiritual eyes opened and saw them. They were there all along, but he had only been going by what he saw with his physical eyes. If Elisha and his servant were limited to only what was true in the physical, they could have been taken by the Syrians.

But because Elisha was basing his faith on what could not be seen by just natural sight, he smote the whole Syrian army with blindness, had them join hands, and then led them to the king of Israel where he opened their eyes again (2 Kgs. 6:18–20). Elisha took the whole army captive because he knew what he had in the spiritual realm.

Likewise, understanding what is going on in the spiritual realm is essential to us receiving the answers to our prayers. God is always faithful to give, but sometimes, it takes a period of time for what God has done in the unseen realm to manifest in the physical realm.

That happened when Jesus spoke to the fig tree in Mark 11:12–14 and 20–24. At the exact moment Jesus cursed the fig tree, it died. But what happened in the roots, below the surface, took twenty-four hours to become visible above ground. The moment we believe we receive in the spirit, it will manifest in the natural, "*if we faint not*" (Gal. 6:9).

Demonic Resistance

There is another great truth I learned through Daniel's two prayers. I used to believe that the devil never missed it. In a way, I was more confident of Satan's resistance than I was of God's faithfulness. But that is totally wrong. Once again, that is not what these scriptures reveal.

There was no demonic resistance against Daniel's prayer in the ninth chapter, but there was massive resistance in the tenth chapter.

Why?

I'm not sure, but this does show that the devil isn't consistent as most people believe he is. He doesn't always fight every prayer. Surprise! The devil isn't perfect, and he's not omniscient.

Maybe he is shorthanded and therefore has to choose which prayers he fights against. Maybe the devil was off licking his wounds when Daniel's first prayer got past him, but after seeing the miraculous prophecy that came forth in Daniel 9, he mustered his forces to oppose Daniel in his second prayer (Dan. 10).

Whatever Satan's reasons were, the difference was the devil and not God or Daniel. I don't think most Christians understand this and therefore just give up if they don't see instant answers. They interpret the lack of physical evidence as proof that God didn't move. That wasn't true in Daniel's case, and it's not true in our cases either.

This demonic resistance that delayed Daniel's prayer was actually a tribute to how powerful Daniel's prayers were. You might say, "How's that?" After seeing the prophecy about the coming of the Messiah in Daniel 9:25–27, Satan determined to try and stop the same thing or something bigger from happening in answer to his prayer in Daniel 10. It was Daniel's miraculous power in prayer that caused Satan to fight him so hard.

Likewise, it's possible that our delay in seeing the manifestation of the answer to our prayers could be because the devil sees us as a threat. He can't stop every answer to prayer, so he picks those who are the biggest threat to his kingdom to fight against.

John 4:24 says that God is a Spirit. He is a spiritual being and lives and moves in the spiritual realm. When He answers our prayers, He gives the command instantly, but there can be time that passes before what He has commanded in the spiritual realm manifests in the physical realm. If we don't understand that, then we can stop our own answers to prayer by giving up before the answer manifests.

Let me give you an illustration of how this can happen.

I had a friend who wanted to sell his house without real estate agent fees, so he put a sign in his yard that read, "For sale by owner." It took two years to sell that house.

He had already moved into a new house while trying to sell his old house, and now he had two mortgages to pay; it was becoming a real financial burden. He couldn't understand why the Lord hadn't sold his house for him. He had prayed about it every day for two years, but nothing seemed to happen.

Then he heard this teaching on what to do when your prayers seem unanswered. He realized the Lord had heard his very first prayer and had moved on someone to buy the house, and it must be the devil that was hindering the sale.

So, the first thing he did was to repent for all the times he had wavered in his belief that the Lord had answered his prayer. He realized the Lord wasn't going to buy the house.

He was going to have some person do that, and so the problem must be on their end.

Since he didn't know who the Lord was speaking to about buying the house, he just decided to pray in tongues and let the Holy Spirit intercede through him for whatever the situation was (Rom. 8:26–27). He spent two days doing that, and then a man came with cash in hand to buy his house.

They went to closing, and as they were sitting at the closing table, the buyer said, "The very first day you put your house on the market, two years ago, I told my wife, 'That is our house.' But I've been hindered for two years getting the money together. Then just two days ago, a man who wanted to buy my house got his house sold and came to me with the money for it, which enabled me to buy your house."

That proved to my friend that the Lord answered his prayer the very first time he prayed, but the devil hindered the answer because other people were involved. What a revelation!

If you own a business, the Lord isn't going to buy your product or use your service. He is going to supply your need through people. As Luke 6:38 says,

Give, and it shall be given unto you; good measure, pressed down, and shaken together, and running over, shall men give into your bosom. ...

Notice that this verse says, "men" will be used in getting this supply to you.

The Lord doesn't have money, and He won't counterfeit it either. The Lord gives you power to get money (Deut. 8:18), but He uses people to deliver it. Anytime other people are involved in your supply, there is potential for the devil using them to slow down or stop the answer to your prayer.

That isn't to say we are completely at the mercy of others. The Lord has given us weapons and authority that Daniel didn't have, but we have to use them. As an Old Testament believer, Daniel didn't have authority over the devil. If Daniel had known that the prince of Persia was hindering his prayer, he couldn't have done anything about it. All he could do was stand in faith and believe the Lord was faithful.

> **The Lord gives you power to get money, but He uses people to deliver it.**

But we, as New Testament believers, have power and authority that puts us in a different situation. Sadly, most believers don't know this or utilize what they have. Therefore, they are not doing anything Daniel didn't do, and they don't see any quicker manifestations. They are just trying to outlast the devil.

When we know we have asked according to His will, we can believe that we receive when we pray (1 John 5:14–15 and Mark 11:24). We can assure our hearts that if we asked, God gave (Matt. 7:7). And if we aren't seeing the visible results of what we prayed for, then it's either our faith wavering (James 1:7) or demonic opposition (Eph. 6:12).

If the problem is that we are wavering in faith, then we can get in the Word because faith comes by hearing God's Word (Rom. 10:17). We can pray in the Spirit and build ourselves up on our most holy faith (Jude 1:20). As our faith is purged of unbelief, we will see what we have prayed for (Matt. 17:20).

If the problem is demonic opposition, then we can do what Daniel couldn't do. We can resist the devil, and he will flee from us (James 4:7).

Resisting the Devil

So, how do we resist the devil?

Praise is a powerful weapon. It not only refocuses our attention away from the problem, but it ushers us into the presence of the Lord (Ps. 22:3 and 100:4). It is also a weapon against the devil that makes him flee.

Jesus said in Matthew 21:16,

…Yea; have ye never read, Out of the mouth of babes and sucklings thou hast perfected praise?

He was quoting from Psalm 8:2, which says,

Out of the mouth of babes and sucklings hast thou ordained strength because of thine enemies, that thou mightest still the enemy and the avenger.

By comparing these two scriptures, you can see that praise is strength to still or stop the enemy and the avenger (i.e., the devil). Satan is the ultimate egomaniac. He can't stand to hear praise to the One who has totally destroyed him. He flees from praise. So, praising God drives the devil away.

And allowing the Holy Spirit to intercede through you in prayer is powerful too.

Romans 8:26 says,

Likewise the Spirit also helpeth our infirmities: for we know not what we should pray for as we ought: but the Spirit itself maketh intercession for us with groanings which cannot be uttered.

The Greek word *sunantilambanomai*, which was translated *helpeth,* literally means, "to take hold of opposite together, co-operate (assist)."[1] The Holy Spirit doesn't intercede without us, and we can't effectively intercede without Him. But there is an intercession where the Holy Spirit takes hold together with us with groanings that can't be uttered. That's when things start to happen.

In 1976, I had a ganglion cyst on my left wrist. I prayed about it and believed it was going to go away, but it seemed to be getting bigger. I wore a wristwatch with an expandable

---

[1] Strong's #4878: Sunantilambanomai - Greek/Hebrew definitions - bible tools. Accessed January 19, 2023. https://www.bibletools.org/index.cfm/fuseaction/Lexicon.show/ID/G4878/sunantilambanomai.htm.

band, which hid the cyst so others couldn't see it, but I knew it was there. I couldn't understand why it wasn't leaving.

This was during the time the Lord was showing me the things I've shared with you in this booklet. It finally dawned on me that the Lord had already answered my prayer. The problem was either me struggling in my faith, or it was just the devil fighting against me.

I started praying in the Spirit to build myself up on my most holy faith (Jude 1:20), and then I got into the Holy Spirit taking hold together with me and interceding against any hindrances the devil might be using against me. I prayed like that till late in the night. I didn't see any difference in the size of the cyst, but I knew I had dealt with whatever the problem was. When I got up in the morning, the cyst was totally gone and has never come back. Praise the Lord!

Instead of just praying and asking the Lord to do something, then waiting forever for the manifestation, we can shorten the time between when we say, "Amen" and "There it is." Daniel couldn't do that. He just had to stand, and stand, and stand. But through the power of the Holy Spirit, we can remove Satan's hindrances to a large degree.

Drawing Out the Power

We don't have authority over people, and if people are involved in our answers to prayer, we have to deal with that. You also can't microwave your ministry. Ministry is tied to maturity, and there is a due season to reaping (Gal. 6:9).

> **You can't microwave your ministry.**

But much of what we are asking for is already ours and just needs to be received. Ephesians 1:3 says,

Blessed be the God and Father of our Lord Jesus Christ, who hath blessed us with all spiritual blessings in heavenly places in Christ.

1 Peter 2:24 says,

…by whose stripes ye were healed.

If we were healed, then we are healed. We have the resurrection power of Christ in our born-again spirits. We just have to draw it out.

Imagine a person who was dying of thirst, but they were leaning against a well that was full of life-giving water. If the person didn't know there was water in the well, or if they didn't know how to draw the water out, they could die of thirst just a few feet away from their answer.

Likewise, we have the supernatural power of God available to us through prayer. But most don't know how to draw it out of the spiritual realm and into the natural realm. There is a spiritual world all around us, and for those who have become new creations through faith in Jesus (2 Cor. 5:17), there is a new you inside of you. We've got everything we need to become victorious sons and daughters of God (John 1:12), but that power has to be known and understood.

The Lord gives us all things that we need in this life through the knowledge of Him, which is revealed in His Word. 2 Peter 1:3–4 says,

> *According as his divine power hath given unto us all things that* pertain *unto life and godliness, through the knowledge of him that hath called us to glory and virtue: Whereby are given unto us exceeding great and precious promises: that by these ye might be partakers of the divine nature, having escaped the corruption that is in the world through lust.*

It's the truth that makes us free (John 8:32), but it's only the truth we know that makes us free. What we don't know is killing us (Hos. 4:6).

In 1973, I was living in Seagoville, Texas, and pastoring a very small church. Jamie and I got behind on our rent because we just didn't have any money. It wasn't a matter of us using our money for other things. We were so broke; we couldn't even pay attention.

I contacted my landlord the day the rent was due and told her I didn't have the money, but I would get it. I was not avoiding her. I told her we were trusting the Lord and believed we would have the money soon. After three weeks, she wrote me a letter mocking my faith. She told me how ungodly I was for not paying my rent on time. It really hurt me. I wanted to pay on time, but we just didn't have it.

Then I got a call from a lady who wanted to take Jamie and me out to eat. We gladly accepted because we hadn't eaten in days. As we were eating, she handed me a check for exactly what we needed to pay our rent and give off of it. I knew it was the answer to my prayer, but although I was thankful, I thought, *Why three weeks late?*

She went on to tell us that the Lord told her to give this to us four weeks before, but she had never given to anyone except the church. She spent four weeks praying about it before she obeyed.

Wow! The Lord spoke to her even before our rent was due. It wasn't God who hadn't moved to answer our prayer. It was the individual He was using who delayed the physical manifestation. I learned a lesson from that.

The next time it looked like we would be unable to pay our rent on time, I started praying for the person the Lord would use to supply that need before the due date.

This won't be the same for everyone who reads this. I'm a minister, and I receive my income from those I minister to (Gal. 6:6–7). If you work a secular job, you will primarily get your money from the work you do. But the Lord meets my needs through my ministry.

So, I had been at my mother's house, painting a bay window for her and interceding for the one the Lord had already spoken to about giving us some money. While I was painting, my mother called and told me she had seen an old friend on her lunch break. The friend told her she had been wanting to bless Jamie and me with an offering, but she didn't know how to get ahold of us. My mother told her we were in town, painting at her house. We connected later that day, and she gave us more than enough money to meet our need.

Conclusion

Just as I've been relating in this booklet, the Lord answered my prayers instantly, but He doesn't give me money directly. It comes through people. I've learned to pray for the people the Lord is going to use and against any demonic hindrances that may be fighting against the manifestations of my answered prayers.

These same insights about how the Lord answers prayers will unlock answered prayer for you. God is faithful to answer every prayer prayed according to the promises of His Word. The problem isn't with God. The problem is either us or a demonic hindrance, and we can deal with both of those problems.

> God is faithful to answer every prayer prayed according to the promises of His Word.

Some complimentary teachings I have that go right along with this:

- *A Better Way to Pray*
- *Spirit, Soul & Body*
- *You've Already Got It*
- *The Word Became Flesh*

These teachings are available free of charge at **awmi.net/video** or for purchase in book, study guide, CD, DVD, or USB formats at **awmi.net/store**.

I encourage you to take advantage of these resources and let us help you start seeing the things that you've prayed for manifest in the natural realm. You won't regret it.

Receive Jesus as Your Savior

Choosing to receive Jesus Christ as your Lord and Savior is the most important decision you'll ever make!

God's Word promises, *"That if thou shalt confess with thy mouth the Lord Jesus, and shalt believe in thine heart that God hath raised him from the dead, thou shalt be saved. For with the heart man believeth unto righteousness; and with the mouth confession is made unto salvation"* (Rom. 10:9–10). *"For whosoever shall call upon the name of the Lord shall be saved"* (Rom. 10:13). By His grace, God has already done everything to provide salvation. Your part is simply to believe and receive.

Pray out loud: "Jesus, I confess that You are my Lord and Savior. I believe in my heart that God raised You from the dead. By faith in Your Word, I receive salvation now. Thank You for saving me."

The very moment you commit your life to Jesus Christ, the truth of His Word instantly comes to pass in your spirit. Now that you're born again, there's a brand-new you!

Please contact us and let us know that you've prayed to

receive Jesus as your Savior. We'd like to send you some free materials to help you on your new journey. Call our Helpline: **719-635-1111** (available 24 hours a day, seven days a week) to speak to a staff member who is here to help you understand and grow in your new relationship with the Lord.

Welcome to your new life!

Receive the Holy Spirit

As His child, your loving heavenly Father wants to give you the supernatural power you need to live a new life. *"For every one that asketh receiveth; and he that seeketh findeth; and to him that knocketh it shall be opened…how much more shall your heavenly Father give the Holy Spirit to them that ask him?"* (Luke 11:10–13).

All you have to do is ask, believe, and receive!

Pray this: "Father, I recognize my need for Your power to live a new life. Please fill me with Your Holy Spirit. By faith, I receive it right now. Thank You for baptizing me. Holy Spirit, You are welcome in my life."

Some syllables from a language you don't recognize will rise up from your heart to your mouth (1 Cor. 14:14). As you speak them out loud by faith, you're releasing God's power from within and building yourself up in the spirit (1 Cor. 14:4). You can do this whenever and wherever you like.

It doesn't really matter whether you felt anything or not when you prayed to receive the Lord and His Spirit. If you believed in your heart that you received, then God's Word promises you did. *"Therefore I say unto you, What things soever ye desire, when ye pray, believe that ye receive them, and ye shall have them"* (Mark 11:24). God always honors His Word—believe it!

We would like to rejoice with you and help you understand more fully what has taken place in your life!

Please contact us to let us know that you've prayed to be filled with the Holy Spirit and to request the book *The New You & the Holy Spirit*. This book will explain in more detail about the benefits of being filled with the Holy Spirit and speaking in tongues. Call our Helpline: **719-635-1111** (available 24 hours a day, seven days a week).

Call for Prayer

If you need prayer for any reason, you can call our Helpline, 24 hours a day, seven days a week at **719-635-1111**. A trained prayer minister will answer your call and pray with you.

Every day, we receive testimonies of healings and other miracles from our Helpline, and we are ministering God's nearly-too-good-to-be-true message of the Gospel to more people than ever. So, I encourage you to call today!

About the Author

Andrew Wommack's life was forever changed the moment he encountered the supernatural love of God on March 23, 1968. As a renowned Bible teacher and author, Andrew has made it his mission to change the way the world sees God.

Andrew's vision is to go as far and deep with the Gospel as possible. His message goes far through the *Gospel Truth* television program, which is available to nearly half the world's population. The message goes deep through discipleship at Charis Bible College, headquartered in Woodland Park, Colorado. Founded in 1994, Charis has campuses across the United States and around the globe.

Andrew also has an extensive library of teaching materials in print, audio, and video. More than 200,000 hours of free teachings can be accessed at **awmi.net**.

Contact Information

Andrew Wommack Ministries, Inc.
PO Box 3333
Colorado Springs, CO 80934-3333
info@awmi.net
awmi.net

Helpline: 719-635-1111 (available 24/7)

Charis Bible College
info@charisbiblecollege.org
844-360-9577
CharisBibleCollege.org

For a complete list of our offices, visit
awmi.net/contact-us.

Connect with us on social media.

Andrew's LIVING COMMENTARY BIBLE SOFTWARE

Andrew Wommack's *Living Commentary* Bible study software is a user-friendly, downloadable program. It's like reading the Bible with Andrew at your side, sharing his revelation with you verse by verse.

Main features:
- Bible study software with a grace-and-faith perspective
- Over 26,000 notes by Andrew on verses from Genesis through Revelation
- *Matthew Henry's Concise Commentary*
- 11 Bible versions
- 2 concordances: *Englishman's Concordance* and *Strong's Concordance*
- 2 dictionaries: *Collaborative International Dictionary* and *Holman's Dictionary*
- Atlas with biblical maps
- Bible and *Living Commentary* statistics
- Quick navigation, including history of verses
- Robust search capabilities (for the Bible and Andrew's notes)
- "Living" (i.e., constantly updated and expanding)
- Ability to create personal notes

Whether you're new to studying the Bible or a seasoned Bible scholar, you'll gain a deeper revelation of the Word from a grace-and-faith perspective.

Purchase Andrew's *Living Commentary* today at **awmi.net/living**, and grow in the Word with Andrew.

Item code: 8350

ANDREW WOMMACK MINISTRIES

CHARIS
BIBLE COLLEGE

God has more for you.

Are you longing to find your God-given purpose? At Charis Bible College you will establish a firm foundation in the Word of God and receive hands-on ministry experience to **find, follow,** and **fulfill** your purpose.

Scan the QR code for a free Charis teaching!

CharisBibleCollege.org
Admissions@awmcharis.com
(844) 360-9577

Change your life. **Change the world.**